For Michael Cohen, drama teacher and friend,
in thanks for your many years of outstanding service at Rosemead High School.

3

Don't Forget Me

SATB Chorus a

Henrik Ibsen (1828–1906), alt. R. M. G.

...rris Gray

C000082692

Duration: approx. 4:00

Also available: Performance/Accompaniment CD (99/2925H).

www.lorenz.com

LT

4

rev-er-ie's_____ rich-col-ored play.

Sleep on,_____ dream-er,

soft and gent-ly, were I_____ made a

2871H ◯ Performance/Accompaniment CD (99/2925H)

Don't Forget Me

Ruth Morris Gray

SATB
Edition

Distinguished
Text
by
Henrik Ibsen

HERITAGE MUSIC PRESS

Distinctive Choral Music *for the* Discriminating Music Educator

A Lorenz Company • www.lorenz.com

Henrik Ibsen (1828–1906) was a major 19th–century Norwegian playwright, theater director, and poet. Many critics consider him to be the greatest playwright since Shakespeare. He is often referred to as the "father of prose drama" and is one of the founders of Modernism in the theater. His most famous works are *Peer Gynt* (1867), *A Doll's House* (1879), and *Hedda Gabler* (1890).

Ibsen wrote poems throughout his life as well, though primarily only up to 1875. After that, he essentially gave up verse as a form of literature. This text was written in1857 to his wife-to-be, Suzannah Thorensen, and titled *To My Rose.*

To My Rose
by Henrik Ibsen

Reverie's rich-colored play Sleep now,
to night's peace surrender,
Sleep whoever will and may,
I shall lull myself in tender.

On the wings of verse I'll send you
Thoughts of mine in soaring flocks,
While hushed sprites of sleep attend you,
Wafting o'er your dark brown locks.

Sleep on, dreamer, soft and gently,
Were I made a child anew,
I would send a prayer to heaven—
Ah, but that's a task for you.

And if you are gently drowsing,
Don't forget me as you doze,
Don't forget the one whose only
Dream is of his lovely rose.

6

thoughts of __ mine in soar - ing flocks; __ Hushed sprites of

sleep at - tend you, waft - ing o'er your dark brown locks. __

o'er your dark brown locks. __

Sleep now, sleep now, dream now, now. __

now. __

dream now. Sleep now, sleep now, dream

now. Sleep now.

now.

And if you are gent - ly drows - ing,

please don't for - get me as you doze,

whose dream is

Don't for - get the one whose on - ly dream is of

HERITAGE MUSIC PRESS

Distinctive Choral Music *for the* Discriminating Music Educator

A Lorenz Company • www.lorenz.com